100

THINGS TO DO IN
SAN ANTONIO
BEFORE YOU
DIE

Tredyffrin Public Library
582 Upper Gulph Road
Strafford, PA 19087
(610) 688-7092 12/16

D0841534

100

THINGS TO DO IN
SAN ANTONIO
BEFORE YOU
DIE

• •

DENISE BARKIS RICHTER, PhD

REEDY PRESS

Copyright © 2016 by Reedy Press, LLC
Reedy Press
PO Box 5131
St. Louis, MO 63139, USA
www.reedypress.com

No part of this publication may be reproduced or transmitted in any form or by any means, electronic or mechanical, including photocopy, recording, or any information storage and retrieval system, without permission in writing from the publisher.

Permissions may be sought directly from Reedy Press at the above mailing address or via our website at www.reedypress.com.

Library of Congress Control Number: 2015957485

ISBN: 9781681060293

Text and photos by Denise Barkis Richter, Ph.D.

Design by Jill Halpin

Printed in the United States of America
16 17 18 19 20   5 4 3 2 1

Please note that websites, phone numbers, addresses, and company names are subject to change or cancellation. We did our best to relay the most accurate information available, but due to circumstances beyond our control, please do not hold us liable for misinformation. When exploring new destinations, please do your homework before you go.

DEDICATION

To my fellow San Antonio, Texas, bloggers, my Readhead Book Group, my teachers, my students, my colleagues, my friends, my mother and father, my siblings, my BFF Amy, and especially my husband and daughter, who let me photograph their food before they dig in.

CONTENTS

● ●

• •

Food and Drink

• •

Music and Entertainment

● ●

• •

PREFACE

I love to travel, and I love to write about traveling. Since my gallivanting budget is limited, I decided to become a tourist in my own town, San Antonio, Texas, which happens to be one of the most beautiful, historic, and romantic cities on the planet.

For more than five years, I've been writing about fun things to do and see in the Alamo City on my blog, sanantoniotourist.net. It makes me happy to receive comments from San Antonio natives who discovered something new through my blog or from visitors who thank me for helping them plan a memorable visit. I moved to San Antonio in 1979 as an 18-year-old freshman in college, and I have grown to love my adopted city. I hope that some of my *amor* for the Alamo City rubs off on you.

It is my sincerest wish that this book will motivate both visitors and natives to make the most of San Antonio. Unplug and explore. *¡Disfrute!* (Enjoy!)

CULTURE AND HISTORY

REMEMBER THE ALAMO

Once while I was traveling through Ireland, my bus driver confessed that he played hooky every time John Wayne's 1960 movie *The Alamo* came on TV. Though the historic mission is tiny in person, its reputation is grand throughout the world. It's the number one travel destination in Texas, and it and San Antonio's four other eighteenth-century Spanish colonial missions are a UNESCO World Heritage Site, the only one in Texas and one of only twenty-three in the U.S. On the Ireland trip, I happened to have a faux coonskin cap with me, and I gave it to the teary-eyed driver. Yes, the Alamo delivers that kind of emotional impact. Don't miss it.

300 Alamo Plaza, 210-225-1391
thealamo.org

MEANDER ALONG
THE RIVER WALK

San Antonio's River Walk, also known as the Paseo del Rio, on the San Antonio River is one of the most beautiful spots in the United States. No brag, just fact. Ask anyone who's been. The day after Thanksgiving through the Feast of the Epiphany in early January has always been my favorite time of year in downtown San Antonio. Twinkle lights in the trees along the River Walk create a magical space that transports you into a different realm. Strolling along the Paseo del Rio in a sea of lights will put even the grinchiest of grinches in a good mood. Throughout the year, you will also enjoy experiencing the river being dyed green for St. Patrick's Day, the Fiesta River Parade, Spurs championship parades, arts & crafts fairs, restaurants, bars, clubs, and shopping, all thanks to architect Robert H.H. Hugman, whose 1929 proposal saved the river from being paved over and used as a storm sewer. Works Progress Administration funds post-Depression sealed the deal. Thank you, FDR.

210-227-4262
thesanantonioriverwalk.com

TAKE IN SAN ANTONIO'S
ART MUSEUMS AND GALLERIES

The Alamo City is blessed with an abundance of art museums and galleries. ARTE ES VIDA (ART IS LIFE) is a bumper sticker you'll see around town. No need to travel to Los Angeles, New York City, London, Paris, or Rome. Chances are we have something by your favorite artist or from your favorite time period right here. If I had to pick visiting just one art museum while I was in town, I'd choose the McNay because I love the setting and the collection; however, being asked to select one museum is like being asked to pick your favorite child. It's too painful. I love them all for different reasons, so please visit all of them.

Artpace, 445 N Main Ave., 210-212-4900
artpace.org

Blue Star Contemporary Art Museum, 116 Blue Star, 210-227-6960
bluestarart.org

Briscoe Western Art Museum, 210 W Market St., 210-299-4499
briscoemuseum.org

McNay Art Museum, 6000 N New Braunfels Ave., 210-824-5368
mcnayart.org

San Antonio Museum of Art, 200 W Jones Ave., 210-978-8100
samuseum.org

Southwest School of Art Exhibition Galleries
300 Augusta Street, 210-224-1848
swschool.org

BROWSE
THE ALAMO CITY'S PUBLIC LIBRARIES

For those of us with kids who've watched the *Spy Kids* movies written and directed by San Antonio native Robert Rodriguez, you'll recognize San Antonio's Central Library in downtown San Antonio as the OSS headquarters in *SK2*. Designed by Mexican architect Ricardo Legoretta, the edifice is known for its enchilada-red exterior. Inside, you'll find computers with free Internet connectivity, a comfortable place to cool off while you peruse magazines and books, an art gallery, a Dale Chihuly glass sculpture titled *Fiesta Tower*, a Fernando Botero horse sculpture, and a mural by esteemed San Antonio artist Jesse Treviño. San Antonio boasts twenty-six branch libraries scattered throughout the city in addition to the Central Library. Landa Branch Library, housed in a 1920s Mediterranean-style mansion at 233 Bushnell, is my favorite. Be sure to enjoy the Carlos Cortés-designed faux bois pavilion in the garden while you're there.

600 Soledad, 210-207-2500
mysapl.org

GET YOUR SPOOK ON
IN DOWNTOWN SAN ANTONIO

Spirits of those who died during the Battle of the Alamo; hotel housekeepers who met an untimely end but are still driven to tidy up; and Captain Richard King, founder of the King Ranch, are all apparitions that you might encounter while on a ghost tour of downtown San Antonio. For those of us who've lived here for a while, tales of La Llorona, the Donkey Lady, and the haunted railroad tracks on the South Side abound, so sign up for a Nightly Ghost Walk Tour by the Sisters Grimm while you're in town to see if you might stumble upon the supernatural. The sisters, descendants of San Antonio's Canary Islands founders, weave tales of the city's history throughout the hour and a half walking tour that covers the Alamo, the Menger Hotel, the Emily Morgan Hotel, San Fernando Cathedral, the Bexar County Courthouse, the Spanish Governor's Palace, the O. Henry House, and Casa Navarro over approximately 2.5 miles.

300 Alamo Plaza, 210-638-1338
sistersgrimmghosttour.com

FEEL THE SPIRIT
AT HOLY REDEEMER CATHOLIC CHURCH

Those who think you can only find gospel music at Baptist churches haven't been to Holy Redeemer, a Catholic church on San Antonio's East Side. I started going to Holy Redeemer back in the 1980s whenever I needed a spirit boost. The choir, backed by an amazing band and organist, would come into the church singing "Hosanna, Blessed Be the Rock of My Salvation," and you could feel the energy. I once brought a friend who grew up in Sweden to Mass at Holy Redeemer, and she turned to me and thanked me halfway through the service. When a woman by the name of Mrs. Ferguson (since deceased) sang, goosebumps would spring up over my entire body. Mrs. Ferguson may be gone, but Holy Redeemer is in good hands. An all-girls choir performed at a recent 9 a.m. Sunday Mass. Holy Redeemer celebrated its one hundredth birthday in 2013, and the historic original church now serves as the narthex of the new sanctuary. All are welcome.

1819 Nevada St., 210-532-5358
holyredeemer-satx.org

STROLL
THROUGH HISTORIC LA VILLITA

San Antonio's La Villita (little village) is the city's original melting pot. Native Americans, Mexicans, Spaniards, East Texans, Texas Rangers, Germans, Swiss, French, and Anglos all called this little piece of land home. Located in the shadow of the Hilton Palacio del Rio along the banks of the San Antonio River on South Alamo at Nueva Streets, La Villita's melting pot heritage lives on today through the countless festivals that are held here each year: Night in Old San Antonio, Soul Food Festival, Diwali: Festival of Light, St. Patrick's Day Festival, Mardi Gras, Fiesta Noche del Rio, and the Diez y Seis Celebration to name a few. My personal favorite is the International Accordion Festival in September that showcases squeezebox talent from all over the world in Maverick Plaza and the Arneson River Theatre. It's free, and it's fun. If you aren't in town for one of these festivals, don't worry. The shops, galleries, restaurants, and Little Church of La Villita offer plenty to do and see.

418 Villita St., 210-207-8614
getcreativesanantonio.com/exploresanantonio/lavillita

IMAGINE LATE NINETEENTH-CENTURY LIFE
IN KING WILLIAM

Surely the spirit of Walter Nold Mathis still roams the dazzling rooms and lovely grounds of his beloved Villa Finale, a grand 1876 Italianate home in San Antonio's King William neighborhood, the first historic neighborhood in Texas. Even if Mathis's spirit doesn't ramble around, his essence definitely lingers on through his immense collection of fine and decorative arts. The Villa Finale is the first National Trust Historic Site in the State of Texas, and Mathis left plenty behind for visitors to enjoy: Napoleonic memorabilia, including a death mask of the French emperor; snuff and match boxes; letter openers; Greek and Russian religious items; sterling silver coffee and tea sets; pewter plates, mugs, and serving pieces; prints by the artist Mary Bonner; bronze statues; Italian paintings; more than two thousand books; and English Wedgwood. Villa Finale is a wonderful example of the magnificent homes in this historic neighborhood built by German immigrants. Both Villa Finale and the Steves Homestead are open for public tours.

kingwilliamassociation.org/kw
villafinale.org
saconservation.org/EducationTours/HistoricalTours

LEAVE YOUR WORRIES BEHIND
AT OUR LADY OF LOURDES GROTTO

San Antonio's Our Lady of Lourdes Grotto is the perfect space to take a deep breath away from life's hustle and bustle. Plus, it's a two-for-one grotto. Besides the Lourdes grotto, an exact replica of the shrine in France, you may also visit the Our Lady of Guadalupe Tepeyac de San Antonio place of prayer and devotion located on top of the Lourdes grotto. Masses at the grotto are Saturdays at 6 p.m., Sundays at 9 a.m. in English and 11:30 a.m. in Spanish, Mondays through Saturdays at 7 a.m. in English, Mondays through Fridays at noon in Spanish, and a Charismatic Mass at 7 p.m. on Thursdays. The rosary is said at 7:30 p.m. on Mondays and Wednesdays. The Oblate School of Theology's grounds are filled with walking paths, shade trees, outdoor Stations of the Cross, and benches. A large gift shop is located near the grotto and is open seven days a week from 10 a.m. to 6 p.m.

5712 Blanco Rd., between Oblate and Parade, 210-342-9864
oblatemissions.org/our-lady-of-lourdes-grotto

VISIT
THE ONLY UNESCO WORLD HERITAGE SITE IN TEXAS

San Antonio's eighteeenth-century Spanish colonial missions—Concepción; San José; San Juan Capistrano; Espada; and San Antonio de Valero, the Alamo—are one of only twenty-three World Heritage Sites in the United States. They share the list with the Grand Canyon, Yellowstone, the Statue of Liberty, and Monticello. In other words, they are a MUST DO thing in San Antonio. Though similar, each mission has its own distinct flavor. Noteworthy items include the Rose Window and grist mill at San José, the arched doorway and aqueduct at Espada, the cloister at Concepción, the demonstration garden at San Juan, and the shrine and Long Barrack at the Alamo. The national park's Visitor Center is located at San José, where the film *Gente de Razon* explains life in the 1700s. The Mission Reach, an eight-mile stretch of the River Walk, makes travelling from mission to mission a breeze.

nps.gov/saan/index
whc.unesco.org/en/list/1466
thealamo.org

BEANNACHTAÍ NA FÉILE PÁDRAIG ORAIBH!
(ST. PATRICK'S DAY BLESSINGS UPON YOU!)

When I traveled through Ireland back in the '80s and '90s and the folks there learned that I lived in San Antonio, Texas, they'd ask, "Say, lassie, is it true that they dye the river green for St. Patrick's Day?" I could say without a trace of blarney that indeed 'tis true. Many soldiers of the famed Battle of the Alamo were Irish. To commemorate their service, members of San Antonio's Harp & Shamrock Society lay a wreath on the shrine at noon on St. Patrick's Day. If the feast day of St. Patrick falls during Lent, don't worry. I have it from good counsel—our Irish priest—that only thirty-nine of the forty days of Lent are observed by those with Irish blood. "You'll be wanting to water the shamrocks" is what he actually said. Durty Nelly's Irish Pub, MadDogs, and Pat O'Brien's all cater to the everyone-is-Irish-for-a-day crowd.

harpandshamrock.org

SIT FOR A SPELL
IN SAN FERNANDO CATHEDRAL

Many believe that the Alamo is the heart of San Antonio, but in reality San Fernando Cathedral wears that crown. Built by the Canary Islands settlers in 1738, an 1828 fire destroyed the church. In 1872, its dome fell in, and in 1921, floodwaters reached as high as the Stations of the Cross. Despite these setbacks, the cathedral remained strong. Jim Bowie was married in San Fernando, and his remains are entombed there along with those of Davy Crockett and William B. Travis. Thanks to the leadership of Phil Hardberger, a former San Antonio mayor, the area in front of San Fernando Cathedral is now a pedestrian-only plaza that leads down to the River Walk. When Pope John Paul II was in San Antonio in the mid-'80s and celebrated Mass at San Fernando, he said he knew he was in the U.S., but he felt that he was in Mexico. The Mexican and Spanish roots of San Antonio are deepest at San Fernando.

archsa.org/parishes/san-fernando-cathedral

PAY YOUR RESPECTS
AT SAN FERNANDO CEMETERY NUMBER TWO

San Fernando Cemetery Number Two covers ninety-two acres of land on San Antonio's West Side. Founded in 1921, the cemetery hosts the remains of Congressman Henry B. Gonzalez and thousands of San Antonio's citizens. The cemetery is filled with vintage tombstones that rival the ones in the famous Père Lachaise Cemetery in Paris, where The Doors' Jim Morrison is buried. Strolling through San Fernando and reading the tombstones, the link to our city's history is palpable. At the end of October/beginning of November, the Aztec tradition of the Day of the Dead (El Día de los Muertos), which celebrates the lives of departed loved ones, is alive and well in the Alamo City. At this cemetery and others, you will find family members spiffing up the graves of their friends and relatives.

746 Castroville Rd., 210-432-2303
archsa.org/catholic-cemeteries

SAN ANTONIO IS CRAWLING WITH DIA DE LOS MUERTOS EVENTS FOR YOU TO ENJOY

- SAY Sí's Annual Muertitos Fest
- The Esperanza Center's Día de los Muertos Celebration
- Market Square's Día de los Muertos Celebration
- La Villita's Día de los Muertos Celebration
- The Guadalupe Cultural Arts Center's Día de los Muertos Celebration

WAVE YOUR BIBLIOPHILE FLAG
AT THE SAN ANTONIO BOOK FESTIVAL

Just when you think that San Antonio can't get any better, a new event is added to the city's long list of hip happenings that makes the Alamo City even more fabulous. The San Antonio Book Festival is that event. Held the first Saturday of April, more than seventy-five authors—local, regional, national, and international—of every genre—children's, young adult, mystery, history, travel, romance and more—are represented at San Antonio's Central Library. The festival offers readings, panel discussions, and book signings galore. Children and teens will enjoy the hands-on activities. The book festival's schedule is extensive, so plan on spending all day from 9:30 a.m. until 5 p.m. Although entry to the festival is free, bring some money along so that you may purchase books from the exhibitor tent and something to eat from local food trucks.

600 Soledad, 210-207-2500
saplf.org/festival

CONNECT WITH NATURE
AT THE SAN ANTONIO
BOTANICAL GARDEN

The San Antonio Botanical Garden is a must-see for both visitors and natives. Even those with the blackest of thumbs will come away hopeful. You'll enter through the Sullivan Carriage House, a jewel of a building designed by noted architect Alfred Giles. The 38-acre spread will give you a taste of Japan, deserts, South Texas, the East Texas Piney Woods, and the Texas Hill Country without having to spend money on gas to get there. Don't miss the Bird Watch Structure given by Bill, Bob, and Elizabeth Lende in honor of John C. Holmgreen. Maybe it's because I grew up in Southeast Texas, but the East Texas Piney Woods area is my favorite spot in the garden. (The Japanese garden runs a close second.) If you have only a limited amount of time to explore, be sure this soothing, pine-scented area is on your agenda. Sit for a spell on the porch of the East Texas Cabin and gaze at the sunning turtles lounging on logs in the tranquil pond.

555 Funston Place, 210-207-3250
sabot.org

LOOKING FOR LOVE?
ASK SAINT ANTHONY FOR HELP!

San Antonio, Texas, is named for St. Anthony of Padua. For those in the know, St. Anthony is the go-to guy for finding lost or stolen items. What you may not know is that St. Anthony is also the go-to guy for finding your true love. In Guatemala, singles flock to area churches on St. Anthony's Feast Day, June 13, to ask him for help in finding their better half. It just so happens that I was in Antigua, Guatemala, on St. Anthony's Feast Day back in 1992. The woman I was boarding with sent me to the church across the street to have a chat with St. Anthony and to place thirteen coins in his offering box. Is it a coincidence that my boyfriend showed up two weeks later with an engagement ring that sparkled with thirteen diamonds? I don't think so. Residents of and visitors to San Antonio can connect with St. Anthony right here in the Alamo City. St. Anthony de Padua Catholic Church was founded to serve the workers and neighbors of Cementville, the area surrounding the Alamo Cement Company's quarry, home of the current Alamo Quarry Market. Inside the church, which also holds a special devotion to Our Lady of Guadalupe, you'll find a relic of St. Anthony encased in a marble stand. Look below the St. Anthony statue to the left of the altar. The prayer chapel out front is the original 1927 church. Outdoor Stations of the Cross beckon visitors.

102 Lorenz Rd., 210-824-1743
stanthonydepadua.org

MORE THAN LIONS AND TIGERS AND BEARS
AT THE SAN ANTONIO ZOO AND AQUARIUM

One of my fondest memories of the San Antonio Zoo and Aquarium is a sleepless night spent camping out with a kinkajou, a nocturnal Brazilian rainforest mammal, and my daughter's Girl Scout troop. I've always thought the San Antonio Zoo and Aquarium is one of the Alamo City's best destinations. The Africa Live! area is a fabulous way to take a vicarious trip to the African continent to learn about its majestic animals and their conservation issues. Other highlights of the fifty-six-acre park include Butterflies! Caterpillar Flight School, Gibbon Forest, Kronkosky's Tiny Tot Nature Spot, TOADally!, Lory Landing, Amazonia, the Hixon Bird House, the Friedrich Aquarium, and the Zootennial Carousel. It will take you more than one day to see all nine thousand of the zoo's amphibians, birds, reptiles, and mammals, so grab a map and wear comfortable walking shoes.

3903 N St. Mary's St., 210-734-7184
sazoo-aq.org

EXPERIENCE
THE MAJESTIC PEACEFULNESS OF THE LITTLE FLOWER BASILICA

San Antonio's Basilica of the National Shrine of the Little Flower is one of only eighty basilicas in the United States. Built during the Great Depression and named for Saint Thérèse of Lisieux, you can't miss the bright yellow spires of the Basilica from Interstate 10 when leaving or entering downtown. Located on the corner of Culebra at Zarzamora, the Roman Catholic church rises majestically above the West Side of San Antonio. Inside, visitors will feel a sense of awe and wonder. St. Thérèse believed that we should do everything in life out of our love for God and our neighbors without expecting any reward or recognition in return. "Miss no single opportunity of making some small sacrifice, here by a smiling look, there by a kindly word; always doing the smallest right and doing it all for love," she said.

1715 N Zarzamora, 210-735-9126
littleflowerbasilica.org

LEARN
ABOUT COWBOYS AND DINOSAURS

The Witte Museum, a perennial favorite because of its dinosaurs, natural history collection, H-E-B Body Adventure, and special exhibits, has added yet another reason to visit. The Robert J. and Helen C. Kleberg South Texas Heritage Center celebrates the history and people of this region. The twenty-thousand-square-foot addition overlooking the San Antonio River brings the stories of Native Americans, Spanish settlers, cowboys/vaqueros, merchants, ranchers, farmers, oilmen and women, and more to life. A sash worn by Republic of Texas President Sam Houston graces one of the displays. Hands-on classes allow visitors to try on the chaps, boots, and hats of cowboys. Actors dressed in period costumes roam around the center telling stories of South Texas. They also stage mini-plays outside at the Will Smith Amphitheater along the river. Don't miss the Julian Onderdonk, Porfirio Salinas, and William Aiken Walker paintings in the Russell Hill Rogers Texas Art Gallery while you're at this Smithsonian-affiliated museum.

3801 Broadway, 210-357-1900
wittemuseum.org

MARDI GRAS?
SCHMARDI GRAS! ¡VIVA FIESTA!

Fiesta San Antonio is a seventeen-day citywide party every April that offers something for everyone: parades, royalty, performing arts, commemorative medals, arts and crafts, colorful cascarones (confetti eggs), cooking competitions, raspas, and more. Launched in 1891 to pay tribute to the heroes of the Alamo and the Battle of San Jacinto, Fiesta now includes more than one hundred nonprofit organizations coordinating many unique events. More than seventy-five thousand volunteers pitch in to make Fiesta happen. The flagship Battle of Flowers Parade is second in size to the Tournament of Roses Parade. The Fiesta Flambeau Parade is the nation's largest illuminated night parade, and the Texas Cavaliers River Parade is unlike any other. Floats float. Night in Old San Antonio, Cornyation, St. Mary's Oyster Bake, the King William Fair, and ninety-six other events make Fiesta something you must experience for yourself. You'll be back for this annual extravaganza! Out-of-towners reserve hotel rooms along the parade routes a year in advance.

facebook.com/FiestaSA
fiesta-sa.org

FIND YOUR MUSE
AT THE SOUTHWEST SCHOOL OF ART

Southwest School of Art is an oasis of serenity in downtown San Antonio. Their brochure says it's an urban oasis, but I don't think that quite captures the spirit of the place. After all, SSA is housed in what was a cloistered convent built in 1851. All the prayers of the Ursuline nuns seeped into the pores of the place, giving it a spiritual air. Pick up a self-guided tour brochure at the center to make sure you hit all of SSA's high points, including the Zilker Courtyard, the chapel, the convent garden with a grotto dedicated to Our Lady of Lourdes, and the River Garden and its wedding-worthy gazebo along the River Walk. SSA boasts four art galleries that are free and open to the public: the Russell Hill Rogers Galleries, the Navarro Lobby Gallery, the *San Antonio Express-News* Photography Gallery, and the Ursuline Hall Gallery. All are open from 9 a.m. to 5 p.m., Mondays through Fridays.

300 Augusta, 210-224-1848
swschool.org

JUMP ON BOARD
VIA'S #7 SIGHTSEER SPECIAL

For the frugal travelers among you, here's a deal you won't want to miss! For $2.75, you may purchase a one-day VIA bus pass that'll chauffeur you from one San Antonio hot spot to another. Your bus driver's name might not be James/Jamie, but just ask him/her to let you off at the next stop. Here are the destinations along VIA's #7 Sightseer Special route, which begins on Market at Presa (downtown near the convention center) headed north or Funston near North New Braunfels (Botanical Garden) headed south:

- La Villita
- The Alamo
- San Antonio Museum of Art
- DoSeum
- Brackenridge Park
- Japanese Tea Garden (Sunken Gardens)
- San Antonio Zoo and Aquarium
- Trinity University
- University of the Incarnate Word
- Central Market
- Witte Museum/South Texas Heritage Center
- Botanical Garden

The one-day pass is also good for unlimited rides on all regular buses, express buses, and streetcars.

viaonlinestore.net

EXPLORE
SAN ANTONIO'S IVORY TOWERS

San Antonio is the seventh-largest city in America and has more than a dozen institutions of higher learning that befit its size: the Alamo Colleges (Northeast Lakeview College, Northwest Vista College, Palo Alto College, San Antonio College, and St. Philip's College), Our Lady of the Lake University, Trinity University, St. Mary's University, Texas A&M University-San Antonio, University of the Incarnate Word, University of Texas at San Antonio, University of Texas Health Science Center San Antonio, and more. Each campus has its own personality, so spend time walking around. Check out the website of each to learn about special happenings and lectures that are open to the public.

Alamo Colleges: alamo.edu
Our Lady of the Lake: ollusa.edu
Trinity: trinity.edu
St. Mary's: stmarytx.edu
Texas A&M-San Antonio: tamusa.edu
Incarnate Word: uiw.edu
University of Texas at San Antonio: utsa.edu
University of Texas Health Science Center: uthscsa.edu

HONOR
MLK'S LEGACY

Dr. Martin Luther King, Jr. surely smiles down from heaven every time he sees the crowd gathered at San Antonio's annual march in his honor. It's one of the largest in the country. Each year on his national holiday more than one hundred fifty thousand people gather to stroll a 2.75-mile route along the East Side of San Antonio. San Antonio celebrates its diversity. Our mayor, Ivy Taylor, is the first African-American female mayor of a major U.S. city. "Dr. King inspired Americans of all colors and creeds to feel that we were part of something bigger, part of an experiment in democracy and freedom that had yet to be fully realized," she said. "He challenged each of us to play a role in fulfilling the promises made by the founding fathers at the creation of the United States of America: 'We hold these truths to be self-evident, that all men are created equal.'" The march reminds each of us to support Dr. King's dream.

sanantonio.gov/mlk

RELEASE YOUR INNER TECHIE
AT GEEKDOM

Geekdom's mission is to "provide an environment where we empower and inspire innovators in order to transform our world for the better." Geekdom, a collaborative coworking space for entrepreneurs, developers, makers, and creatives, was founded by Graham Weston of Rackspace and Nick Longo of CoffeeCup Software. It provides geeks and wannabees a chance to mingle and learn from each other and perhaps launch the next big tech innovation. My San Antonio Bloggers group has met at Geekdom a couple of times for all-day workshops, and it's a chill space located in the historic Rand Building in downtown San Antonio. Luddites need not worry. Every member of Geekdom must give one hour a week back to another member or do a workshop once a month on their expertise. In other words, it's their mission to make you more tech savvy.

110 E Houston St., 210-373-6730
geekdom.com/events

IMMERSE YOURSELF
IN MILITARY HISTORY AT
FORT SAM HOUSTON

In operation since 1879, Fort Sam is a National Historic Landmark and one of the Army's oldest installations, with more than nine hundred buildings. Geronimo, Teddy Roosevelt, Gen. John "Black Jack" Pershing, and President Dwight D. Eisenhower are all part of its history. Fort Sam's Museum at 2310 Stanley Road is open Tuesdays through Saturdays from 10 a.m. until 4 p.m. The Quadrangle, a visitor favorite, is full of deer, peacocks, ducks, and geese that roam beneath an 1876 clock tower. The Quadrangle is open from 9 a.m. until 6 p.m., Mondays through Fridays, and from noon to 6 p.m. on the weekends. Bring a photo ID for entrance into Fort Sam, and bring quarters to buy pellets to feed the birds and deer. Admission is free. Enter through the Walters Street visitor gate west of Interstate 35.

Fort Sam Houston Visitors Center, Building 4179, 210-221-9205
nps.gov/nr/travel/tx/tx39

TAKE A SPIN
IN A HORSE-DRAWN CARRIAGE
THROUGH DOWNTOWN

San Antonio, Texas, is one of the most romantic cities on the planet. Aside from the San Antonio River Walk, which is perfect for strolling hand-in-hand with your *amor*, the Alamo City also offers horse-drawn carriage rides to take you and your sweetie for *una vuelta* around downtown. The Yellow Rose Carriage Company has been in business since 1982, and it's no coincidence that Valentine was the name of the company's first horse. Lone Star Carriage Company has been in business since 1981, and their slogan is "Let's horse around in San Antonio!" Bluebonnet Carriage Company was founded in 2005, and their mission is to make the ordinary truly extraordinary. According to their website, their Valentine's package includes a twenty-minute tour of downtown, a cozy blanket for snuggling, a long-stemmed rose, and a box of chocolates. Sign me up! Dark chocolates, please. I'll bring the champagne. You may find the horse-drawn carriages across from the Menger Hotel, adjacent to the Alamo.

yellowrosecarriage.com
lonestarcarriage.com
bluebonnetcarriage.com

CATCH THE STARS
AT THE SCOBEE EDUCATION CENTER
AT SAN ANTONIO COLLEGE

Named for Francis Richard "Dick" Scobee, a former student of SAC who became a U.S. astronaut, the twenty-two-thousand-square-foot Scobee Education Center gives visitors a hands-on opportunity to experience space. The $12 million center includes the Scobee Planetarium and the Challenger Learning Center. The planetarium is open to the public most Friday evenings with age-specific programs for children ages four and above that are reasonably priced. The Challenger Learning Center offers simulated missions to the International Space Station for middle school students on science- and math-related field trips. The Scobee Education Center also offers free star-gazing parties throughout the year. Its $25,000 telescope in the Charles E. Cheever, Jr. Star Tower will bring the stars within your reach.

1819 N Main Ave., 210-486-0103
facebook.com/scobeeplanetarium

GET YOUR GREEN ON
AT ECO CENTRO

Now every day is Earth Day in the Alamo City, thanks to the William R. Sinkin Eco Centro, a sustainability outreach center. Named for Bill Sinkin, a San Antonio College alumnus and clean energy champion, the center's goal is to equip the citizens of this region with information on how to achieve a more sustainable lifestyle. Eco Centro, a thirty-one-hundred-square-foot LEED-certified building, gives San Antonio residents and visitors a place to gather and learn how to protect and heal our planet. Hands-on classes include water catchment, organic gardening, composting, tree care, green building, vermiculture, and xeriscaping. When you're at Eco Centro, be sure to take in the sixty-three-foot-long outdoor mural created by Tobin Hill resident Luis Lopez. The artist paid homage to the Native Americans who lived in the area surrounding nearby San Pedro Springs more than twelve thousand years ago.

1802 N Main Ave., 210-486-0417
facebook.com/EcoCentro1

AMBLE AROUND
EL MERCADO

El Mercado (Market Square), a downtown landmark within walking distance of the River Walk, is filled with shops, restaurants, and art galleries. Situated across from Milam Park and the Children's Hospital of San Antonio, this outdoor plaza, coined "The Heartbeat of Mexico," hosts a variety of festivals, such as Cinco de Mayo, Día de Los Muertos, and Fiesta del Mercado, throughout the year. El Mercado boasts of being the largest Mexican market in the United States. Mi Tierra Café y Panaderia with its full bar and bakery has been in business since 1941 and is open twenty-four hours a day. Don't miss their Mexican fudge. Christmas lights make every day a holiday at Mi Ti's. Add in roaming mariachis, and you've got yourself a party. La Margarita Mexican Restaurant and Oyster Bar and Viva Villa Taquería are additional El Mercado options for the hungry and thirsty.

marketsquaresa.com

EXPERIENCE SPANISH COLONIAL LIFE
AT THE GOVERNOR'S PALACE

When a friend from Spain visited San Antonio, I made it a point to tour the Spanish Governor's Palace, a National Historic Landmark located in downtown San Antonio across the street from city hall, with him. Spain's roots in San Antonio are deep. The palace served as the headquarters of the Presidio San Antonio de Bexar's captain and then the home of the Spanish governors. Completed in 1749, it is one of Texas's oldest residences. Don't think Versailles, though. It's very small by today's mega mansion standards. Guests will be able to tour the captain's office and home, a living area, a children's bedroom, a dining room, a kitchen, and a loft. My favorite area, however, is the back patio and courtyard. The stone walls, arched patio, and lovely fountain provide a peaceful respite from downtown's hustle and bustle. For a country that's so new, it's nice to have a piece of history in San Antonio that predates the Declaration of Independence.

105 Plaza de Armas, 210-224-0601
nps.gov/nr/travel/american_latino_heritage/Spanish_Governors_Palace
spanishgovernorspalace.org

MARVEL
IN THE ARCHITECTURE
THAT IS THE TOWER LIFE BUILDING

When I moved to San Antonio in 1979, the building that made me feel I was no longer in a small town but in a big city was the Tower Life Building, which opened in 1929. Designed by famed San Antonio architects Ayres & Ayres, the eight-sided, thirty-story downtown building gave me a New York City vibe. It still does. Positioned along the San Antonio River, I'd often admired the building's gargoyles while walking along the River Walk, but I'd never been inside the building until I took a downtown walking tour over the holidays. The lobby sported a beautiful, tall Christmas tree, but most noteworthy was its snowflake ceiling. The Tower Life's copper roof, green with patina, gives the building its character as does its one-hundred-foot flagpole that displays the American flag. When the tower is lit up at night, it demands that you take a look. Go ahead. Look.

310 S St. Mary's St., 210-554-4444
towerlife.com

STEP INTO HISTORY
AT THREE DOWNTOWN SITES

This is cheating, but I'm giving you this item as a three-for-one since they are all close to each other. (You may also want to include the Spanish Governor's Palace in this visit. See page 34.) The zero mile marker for the Old Spanish Trail sits on city hall's square. This movement was organized in the 1920s to promote a paved highway across the southern portion of the U.S. It's now known as Interstate 10. Famed short story writer O. Henry—William Sydney Porter—lived in a tiny house on the corner of Dolorosa at Laredo in 1885 when he was twenty-three years old. Two of his stories, "A Fog in Santone" and "The Higher Abdication," are set in the Alamo City. The Casa Navarro State Historic Site was the adobe and limestone home of José Antonio Navarro, a signer of the Declaration of Independence for Texas. Visitors will learn about the life and times of this Tejano patriot.

oldspanishtrailcentennial.com
ohenryhouse.org
visitcasanavarro.com

TOUR PUBLIC ART
IN SAN ANTONIO'S WEST SIDE

Since 1994, San Anto Cultural Arts program has identified, trained, and mobilized local artists, both young and old, to create large-scale murals that enliven and help educate the city's urban core. Docent-led or self-guided tours bring the stories, hopes, and dreams of the area's residents to life. The importance of education, *familia*, and Chicano/Chicana culture are on vivid display. If you don't have time to tour all fifty murals, here are five you should definitely check out:

Educación (1994), 2121 Guadalupe at South Chupaderas
8 Stages of the Life of a Chicana (1995), 1303 Tampico at Trinity
Mano a Mano (1999), 1927 West Commerce at North Pinto
Piedad (2003), 1204 Buena Vista at Colorado
Líderes de la Comunidad (2006), 1204 Buena Vista at Colorado

2120 El Paso, 210-226-7466
sananto.org/mural-map.html

EXPLORE YOUR HERITAGE
AT THE INSTITUTE OF TEXAN CULTURES

The University of Texas at San Antonio's Institute of Texan Cultures celebrates the diverse ethnicities and settlement groups that have made Texas great: Belgian, Swiss, Filipino, Hungarian, Polish, Wendish, German, Irish, Jewish, Lebanese, Syrian, Anglo, Chinese, Dutch, English, French, Greek, Italian, Scottish, Czech, Japanese, Native American, Tejano, African-American, Danish, Norwegian, Swedish, Spanish, and Mexican. Hour-long guided tours of the ITC museum are available to the public along with an archive, library, and photo collection for family history research. For more than forty years, the Institute has been hosting its annual Texas Folklife Festival, the biggest cultural celebration in Texas. More than forty cultural groups celebrate their heritage through food, music, dance, arts, and craft. It's one of San Antonio's best events. Put it on your bucket list! It will become an annual event for you.

801 E César E Chávez Blvd., 210-485-2300
texancultures.com

EMBRACE DIVERSITY
AT AN EAST SIDE JEWEL

San Antonio has more than its fair share of performing arts spaces: the Majestic, the Empire, the Tobin Center for the Performing Arts, the Alamodome, the AT&T Center, Trinity University's Laurie Auditorium, the Lila Cockrell Theatre, and more. The Carver Community Cultural Center on San Antonio's East Side, however, may give you the biggest bang for your performing arts buck. Why? The Carver, which emphasizes African and African-American culture, seats six hundred. In a place this size, you are able to see the performers, the costumes, and the sets without binoculars. So, for local folks who've never been to the Carver or for out-of-town folks who are looking for something to do while you're in town, check out their annual season lineup. The Carver, a five-minute cab ride from downtown hotels, is known for bringing both national and international performers in to celebrate the diverse cultures of our world. For those who are driving themselves, parking is free!

226 N Hackberry, 210-207-7211
thecarver.org

LEARN
ABOUT THE CONSEQUENCES
OF DISCRIMINATION AND APATHY

Since 1975, the Jewish Federation's Community Relations Council has offered Holocaust education to students of this region. Their mission is to educate the community about the dangers of hatred, prejudice, and apathy. In 2000, the Holocaust Memorial Museum opened its doors to the general public for self-guided tours. School groups and scheduled groups of fifteen or more are given a docent-led tour and the opportunity to learn from a local Holocaust survivor. Admission is free, but donations are encouraged. Learn about the Nazi rise to power, the concentration camps, and America's soldiers who liberated the survivors. An exterior contemplative area memorializes the six million who died.

12500 NW Military Highway, 210-302-6807
hmmsa.org

TAKE IN A PERFORMANCE
OR TAKE A CLASS AT THE GUADALUPE

Founded in 1980 in the historic 1940 Teatro Guadalupe that sits deep in the heart of San Antonio's West Side, the Guadalupe Cultural Arts Center hosts a treasure trove of Chicano/Chicana arts programming and classes in six major areas: visual arts, music, literature, film, theater, and dance. I took a writing class at the Guadalupe from then-unknown Sandra Cisneros not long after her book *The House on Mango Street* was published. Great teacher. Great class. San Antonio CineFestival, the Tejano Conjunto Festival, the Guadalupe Dance Company, the Inter-American Book Fair and Literary Festival, Hecho a Mano arts and crafts bazaar, and more bring Hispanic heritage and culture to life throughout the year. While you're there, don't miss *La Veladora of Our Lady of Guadalupe*, a forty-foot outdoor mosaic sculpture by local artist Jesse Treviño, who also designed the mosaic mural on the Children's Hospital of San Antonio across from El Mercado.

723 S Brazos St., 210-271-3151
guadalupeculturalarts.org

GET IN TOUCH
WITH YOUR SPIRITUAL SIDE

Although San Antonio's population is one-third Roman Catholic, the religion of the Spaniards who settled here in the early 1700s, Protestant, Jewish, Sikh, Baha'i, Buddhist, Eastern Catholic, Greek Orthodox, Hindu, Muslim, Quaker, and Unitarian congregations abound to help you develop your personal value system and explore the meaning of life.

Baha'i: sanantoniobahai.org
Buddhist: watdhammabucha.us and sanantonio.shambhala.org
Coptic Orthodox: stantonychurch.org
Eastern Catholic: stgeorgesa.org
Jewish: jfsatx.org/community-directory
Greek Orthodox: stsophiagoc.org
Hindu: hindutemplesatx.org
Muslim: icsaonline.org
Nondenominational: celebrationcircle.org
Protestant: sachamber.org/cwt/external/wcpages/relocation/worship.aspx
Quaker: sanantonioquakers.org
Roman Catholic: archsa.org/parishes
Sikh: sikhcenter.us
Unitarian: uusat.org

CRUISE ALONG THE SAN ANTONIO RIVER
TO SOAK UP THE CITY'S HISTORY

Venice, Italy, isn't the only city you may traverse by boat. San Antonio has its own river taxis and tours to spirit you away. Knowledgeable drivers will give you the 411 on local points of interest. Open from 9 a.m. until 9 p.m. daily, Rio San Antonio's taxi passes are good for twenty-four hours and have stops at thirty-nine spots along the San Antonio River. The river tour takes approximately an hour and travels along the horseshoe bend of the river. All the river barges are ADA accessible. Charters are available for groups, corporate outings, and dinner. Some restaurants provide Community Dinner Cruises that may be reserved by the seat for small parties. My absolute favorite time of year to jump on a river taxi is during the holidays from the day after Thanksgiving through the sixth of January. Twinkling colored lights in trees along the river create a magical fairyland that will transport you into another dimension.

800-417-4139 or 210-244-5700
riosanantonio.com

BE INSPIRED
BY VISUAL ARTISTS, POETS, DANCERS, ACTORS, AND SINGERS AT LUMINARIA

In addition to being known as a history hub, a culinary capital, and a geek incubator, San Antonio is also known as a city that values artists and their art. In 2008, former Mayor Phil Hardberger and a team of volunteers established Luminaria, a contemporary arts festival, to showcase San Antonio's artists while illuminating dark sections of downtown. Inspired by *Nuit Blanche* in Paris and *Noche Blanca* in Madrid, Hardberger envisioned a nighttime, multifaceted event here in the Alamo City, and he got it: pop-up exhibition spaces that showcase the work of visual artists, performances by theatrical and dance troupes, film screenings, live music, light projections, murals, poetry readings, and more. The amount of creativity on display will blow you away and make you feel good about being a human. It will also inspire you to make your own art, whatever that art might be. Now staged on two nights each fall, this free event is not to be missed.

luminariasa.org

EXPOSE YOURSELF
TO PHOTOGRAPHIC ART
AT FOTOSEPTIEMBRE

For more than twenty years, the Alamo City has hosted an eclectic and inclusive community-wide celebration of photography during the month of September. On average, forty exhibits are displayed each year at venues throughout San Antonio and the Texas Hill Country. Though the work of local and national artists is included, this platform for photography-based artists is international in scope. Artists from Mexico, Taiwan, Iran, Peru, Japan, Switzerland, France, Poland, the Canary Islands, the Czech Republic, and more have been featured in its solo and group shows. Every photographer—from amateurs to professionals—has equal opportunity to participate. In addition to the physical exhibitions during the month-long celebration, Fotoseptiembre presents curated monographs in their web galleries, where artists' work may be viewed year-round.

fotoseptiembre.com

FOSTER
A LIFETIME LOVE OF LEARNING
AT THE DOSEUM

Since the last time I visited the San Antonio Children's Museum was in 2002 when it was located on Houston Street and my daughter was in preschool, I was intrigued by all the buzz in my bloggers group from moms with children in the zero-to-ten age range. "It's our new favorite place," said one. "We LOVE it!" said another. So, I had to go see it for myself, and I now understand all the accolades. It's awesome, and it's HUGE. Even though I'm not a child, I had fun skipping up the piano-key stairs, pretending that I was a member of the stranded Robinson family in the outdoor tree house, and learning about how different lights change the colors that we see. I also enjoyed chatting with a young girl who was happily engaged in creating a spy kitty mask in the DoSeum's Art Studio. Arts, science, technology, engineering, math, and literacy are all featured in this $47 million hands-on museum.

2800 Broadway, 210-212-4453
thedoseum.org

VISIT THE COUNTY SEAT
OF SAN ANTONIO DE BÉXAR

The 1896 Romanesque Revival–style Bexar (pronounced "bear") County Courthouse sits on the edge of Main Plaza, its Texas granite and red sandstone exterior an eye-catching contrast to the limestone of nearby San Fernando Cathedral. A seven-story cupola shaped like a beehive beckons visitors to this Texas Historic Landmark that's also listed on the National Register of Historic Places. A $23 million multiyear renovation completed in 2015 has restored the seat of county government to architect James Riely Gordon's original vision, including a two-story district courtroom with a coffered ceiling, gilded plaster moldings and capitals, longleaf pine floors, and fifteen decorative windows. Don't forget to look down, though, when you're in the courthouse. The mission tile floors are a thing of beauty.

100 Dolorosa, 210-335-2011
bexar.org

RECHARGE YOUR *QÌ*
(LIFE FORCE) ON THE SPIRIT REACH
OF THE SAN ANTONIO RIVER

The headwaters of the San Antonio River are located in the protected fifty-three-acre Headwaters Sanctuary established by the Sisters of Charity of the Incarnate Word, who came to San Antonio in 1869 to care for victims of a massive cholera epidemic. The native people called the springs Yanaguana, a Coahuiltecan word that means Spirit Waters, and they once gushed twenty feet into the air. Located near the center of San Antonio, this sanctuary provides city-weary visitors a chance to meander along trails and connect with mighty oak trees, native plants, and wildlife that includes more than one hundred species of birds. The sanctuary also provides volunteers an opportunity to restore the ecosystem health of this sacred space. Parking is ticket-free on Fridays, Saturdays, and Sundays near the University of the Incarnate Word's baseball fields. Look for a toolshed and a "Welcome to the Headwaters Sanctuary" banner.

4503 Broadway (GPS: 29.4698, -98.4708), 210-828-2224, ext. 280
headwaters-iw.org

TAKE A SENTIMENTAL JOURNEY
THROUGH THE TOILET SEAT
ART MUSEUM

Aside from our beloved San Antonio Spurs and the Alamo, it's possible that no other San Antonio treasure has garnered as much national attention as folk artist Barney E. Smith. His Toilet Seat Art Museum has been featured on *The View*, *Montel Williams*, the *CBS Morning Show* and in more than fifty magazines and books. Smith, a retired master plumber who was born in 1921, has been making his one-of-a-kind creations for more than fifty years. One of his 1,181 (and counting) seats exhibits a piece of the Challenger Space Shuttle that washed ashore. My favorite seat is one he made for Velma Louise, his wife of seventy-six years. It reads, TO MY SWEETHEART and features a big red heart carved onto a tree with I LOVE YOU and BES/VLS. Admission to the museum is by appointment only. Mr. Smith doesn't charge an entry fee, but he will accept donations to help cover the cost of his art supplies.

239 Abiso Ave., 210-824-7791 by appointment only
facebook.com/Barney-Smiths-Toilet-Seat-Art-Museum-258301387544372

FOOD AND DRINK

ENJOY A BIRD'S-EYE HAPPY HOUR
FROM THE TOWER OF THE AMERICAS

My love affair with San Antonio began in 1968 when my parents took one of my brothers and me to the World's Fair, HemisFair, to soak up the region's confluence of civilizations and to celebrate San Antonio's 250th birthday. All these years later, there's even more reason to love San Antonio. Name another place where you can enjoy a $5 glass of wine with a breathtaking 360-degree view. Happy Hour at the Tower of the Americas is celebrated Monday through Friday from 4:30 p.m. to 7 p.m. If you are headed up to the Happy Hour, make sure you get in the elevator line for the Chart House Restaurant, which also happens to be a romantic dinner destination. Another queue is for the Observation Deck. The 750-foot tower designed for the World's Fair by famed local architect O'Neil Ford is the tallest building in San Antonio. Ford also designed Trinity University's tower.

739 E Cesar Chavez Blvd., 210-223-3101
toweroftheamericas.com

QUENCH YOUR THIRST
AT THE LONGEST BAR IN TEXAS

When my husband and I bellied up to the one-hundred-foot wooden bar at The Esquire Tavern, the gentleman standing next to us said that he owns a T-shirt from the establishment's earlier days that reads, "I got frisked at The Esquire." Frisking no longer takes place, but it's the colorful history of this place that makes for interesting conversation. Founded in 1933 on the day Prohibition was recalled, The Esquire has been a mainstay of downtown San Antonio's thirsty crowd for nearly eighty years. The owners claim that it's the oldest bar on the San Antonio River Walk, and who can disprove them? The Esquire bills itself as a Gastro Pub that serves comfort food. They're also a big force behind San Antonio's cocktail culture, so figure out ahead of time whether you want your apéritif shaken or stirred.

155 E Commerce St., 210-222-2521
esquiretavern-sa.com

BECOME A BREAKFAST TACO BELIEVER

Whenever I travel outside of San Antonio, I most enjoy returning home to breakfast tacos. Those who live here get it. Those who don't live here don't know what they're missing. San Antonio, Texas, is not only the capital of Tex-Mex cuisine but is also the undisputed capital of breakfast tacos. We have an embarrassment of riches. Corn or flour tortillas? Eggs or not? Potatoes? Bacon, ham, or sausage? With or without cheese? Barbacoa? Guacamole? So many options! Personally, I find a migas taco with cheese on a corn tortilla and the perfect amount of salsa quemada a life-affirming experience.

TOP 10 BREAKFAST TACO PICKS

Blue Moon Cafe
facebook.com/Blue-Moon-Cafe-117889961570317

El Milagrito Cafe
elmilagritocafe.com

Mendez Café
facebook.com/pages/Mendez-Cafe/1401964606743670

Panchito's Mexican Restaurant
panchitos.net

Paulina's Mexican Restaurant
facebook.com/Paulinas-Mexican-
Restaurant-177177872329268

Pete's Tako House
petestakohouse.com

Taco Cabana
tacocabana.com

Lee's El Taco Garage
facebook.com/Lees-El-Taco-Garage-95827272905

Taco Taco Café
tacotacosa.com

Teka Molino
tekamolino.com

GET ON BOARD
THE BBQ WAGON

Sliced beef brisket is one place where my family falls off the eat-no-red-meat wagon. When it comes to brisket that's been smoked to perfection and sliced into thin, toothsome strips, our willpower fades away. Sliced beef BBQ must be woven into native Texans' DNA, so we're helpless to its powerful pull. Smoked brisket should be acknowledged for the best smell the Alamo City produces. If only it could be bottled and sold! You could do a two-week vacation in San Antonio and not hit all the BBQ joints in town, but you could try!

HERE'S AN ALPHA LIST OF A DOZEN RECOMMENDATIONS

Augie's Barbed Wire
augiesbbq.com

The Barbecue Station
barbecuestation.com

B&B Smokehouse
bbsmokehouse.com

B&D Ice House
banddicehouse.com

The Big Bib BBQ
thebigbib.com

Bill Miller Bar-B-Q
billmillerbbq.com

Blanco BBQ
blancobbq.com

Bolner's Meat Market
bolnersmeatmarket.com

Ed's Smok-N-Q
edssmoknq.com

Rudy's Country Store and Bar-B-Q
rudysbbq.com

Smoke Shack
smokeshacksa.com

The Smokeouse
thesmokehousebbqsa.com

LEAVE NO PALETA UNTRIED

When the temperature tops one hundred degrees, load the biggest ice chest you own into your car or onto a VIA bus and head on over to El Paraiso Original Ice Cream, also known as *paletas*. Founded in 1984, this family-owned business was the first paleta factory in San Antonio, and the Floreses produce more than ten thousand paletas a day. Strawberry is their number one seller followed by lemon. Coconut and chocolate are tied for third, and vanilla/raisin comes in fourth. Other flavors include banana, mango, tamarind, pecan, pineapple, piña colada, horchata, cantaloupe, cookies and cream, watermelon, pickles, lucas (sweet and sour), cheesecake, and coffee cappuccino. One paleta will set you back fifty cents. If you buy twenty-five at a time, you'll pay forty-four cents per paleta. You'll have a hard time finding a sweeter deal in the Alamo City!

1934 Fredericksburg Rd., 210-737-8101
elparaisoicecream.com

SO MANY CUPCAKES,
SO LITTLE TIME

Bird Bakery is called "the nest" by its employees. Aside from its adorable atmosphere, their food is to die for. Owners Elizabeth Chambers, who was born in San Antonio, and her husband, the actor Armie Hammer, opened Bird in March 2012. When I took the first bite of my tarragon chicken salad sandwich and gave Elizabeth a big thumbs up, she said, "I'm so happy you like it." The real reason to visit Bird Bakery, however, is their cupcakes: carrot, red velvet, The Elvis, chocolate peanut butter, sea salt caramel, chocolate, lemon, fresh coconut, coconut candy bar, nostalgic yellow, decadent chocolate, black and white, blue vanilla, pink vanilla, chocolate strawberry, and fresh strawberry. You'll want to give their cakes, pies, cookies, brownies, lemon squares, and pecan bars some attention too. Yes, it will take a bit of effort for you to make it through all of these, but I have faith that you can do it!

5912 Broadway, 210-804-2473
birdbakery.com

WHAT'S NOT TO BE HAPPY
ABOUT A $1.50 MARGARITA?

San Antonio is awesome for many reasons, but one of the most awesome has to be $1.50 margaritas during Taco Cabana's Happy Hour every day from 4 p.m. to 7 p.m. Seriously. A buck fifty. Throw in a plate of bean and cheese nachos for $1.49 and you've got a $3 Happy Hour. Awesome? *¡Por cierto!* (For sure!) Taco Cabana's salsa bar sets it apart from most Mexican restaurants. By adding pico de gallo, cilantro, your choice of salsas, and a splash of lime, your plain bean and cheese nachos will become a work of art. For out-of-towners new to Tex-Mex, you haven't truly lived until you've eaten one of Taco Cabana's bean and cheese tacos. Recently, I've become addicted to Taco Cabana's black bean tacos on corn tortillas, which contain about half the calories of flour tortillas. With close to forty locations in San Antonio, Taco Cabana is right around the corner.

tacocabana.com

FIND OUT
WHETHER OR NOT YOU'RE MACHO

Voted the *San Antonio Express-News* Readers' Choice for best non-chain, local burgers again and again, Chris Madrid's has had an extremely loyal following since 1977 when it opened in a converted gas station. Where else are hungry patrons content to wait in a line that crosses the restaurant? Their motto is "Cook Each Item as if You Were Cooking it for a Friend," and you can feel the love. Chris's tostada burger is what lures us in. Homemade refried beans, chips, onions, and cheddar cheese top a quarter-pound (regular) burger or a half-pound (macho) burger. You'll want to stop by their salsa bar to add a little heat to your selection. Plus, don't skip the fries (regular or macho). They are the real deal. Be sure to get at least two napkins per person. The tostada burger is a gooey mess, but, boy, is it good.

1900 Blanco Rd., 210-735-3552
chrismadrids.com

GRAZE YOUR WAY
ACROSS CENTRAL MARKET

Central Market is the H-E-B grocery store chain's gift to San Antonio's citizens and visitors. Just walking into Central Market makes me happy. Buying a bar of dark chocolate from Ghana makes me even happier. Taking in the abundance of fresh-cut flowers and stunning variety of fruits and vegetables practically makes me swoon. A wonderful thing about Central Market is that you can snack your way across continents for free. (I'm a Spanish cheese addict, I admit.) Everyone in your party will be sure to find something wonderful to eat and drink. Choosing will be the problem. The selection is tremendous. The store also features chef-prepared dinners for two for $15 or less. How great is that? While you're in the store, pick up something to bring home that'll remind you of your fabulous trip to San Antonio: a package or two of flour tortillas, Texas BBQ sauce, or pecan-flavored coffee called "Taste of San Antonio," for example.

4821 Broadway, 210-368-8600
centralmarket.com

DO THE TIME WARP
AT DEWESE'S TIP TOP CAFE

My husband and I met a friend who graduated from nearby Thomas Jefferson High School in 1960 for dinner at DeWese's Tip Top Cafe. When we got to the restaurant, Tony said, "Welcome to the time warp." In all the years he's been eating at the Tip Top, it hasn't changed. Why ruin a good thing? Winnie and Pappy DeWese started the family-owned restaurant in 1938, and their granddaughter, Linda DeWese, has carried on. The Tip Top gives its loyal customers what they crave: tried-and-true comfort food. All the food is tasty, but the onion rings alone are worth a trip. Like Earl Abel's, another San Antonio time-warp restaurant, the Tip Top has pies galore to top off your meal. Or if you just want a little something sweet, pick up an Aunt Aggie De's Praline or two when you're checking out. They've been named the Official Best Gourmet Praline and Pecan Candy in Texas.

2814 Fredericksburg Rd., 210-732-0191
tiptopcafe.com

TRAVEL VICARIOUSLY
IN SAN ANTONIO, TEXAS

You won't need a passport to enjoy international cuisine in San Antonio, Texas, which is fast becoming one of America's leading culinary capitals. Give the food at these international establishments a taste. Bon appétit!

Chico's Bakery (Mexico)
facebook.com/pages/Chicos-Bakery

Demo's Greek Food (Greece)
demosgreekfood.com

España Bar de Tapas (Spain)
espanabar.com

Frederick's (France)
frederickssa.com

The Fruteria (Mexico)
chefjohnnyhernandez.com/thefruteria

Hot Joy (Asian fusion)
hotjoysa.com

Hung Fong Chinese Restaurant (China)
facebook.com/HungFongSA

India Oven (India)
indiaoven.biz

La Frite Belgian Bistro (Belgium)
lafritesa.com

Paesanos (Italy)
paesanositalianrestaurant.com

Paloma Blanca (Mexico)
palomablanca.net

Pasha Mediterranean Grill (Mediterranean)
gopasha.com

Pho Sure Vietnamese Restaurant (Vietnam)
pho-sure.com

Picante Grill (Mexico)
picantegrill.com

Schilo's Delicatessen (Germany)
schilos.com

Simi's India Cuisine (India)
simisindiacuisine.com

WELCOME
TO SAN ANTONIO, THE KING AND QUEEN OF TEX-MEX CUISINE!

People who've lived in San Antonio and have had to move away never fail to lament the lack of excellent Tex-Mex food in their new city. The first thing they do when they get back to San Antonio is visit their favorite restaurants. Enchiladas, carne guisada, chalupas, fajitas, refried beans, rice, nachos, flautas, salsa and chips, tacos al pastor, queso, guacamole . . . you can't go wrong! Here's an alpha list to help you eat your way across our fair city, and don't forget to check out the breakfast tacos list of restaurants on page 55.

Casa Rio
casa-rio.com

Don Pedro
donpedro.net

El Mirador
elmiradorrestaurant.com

La Fogata
lafogata.com

La Fonda on Main
lafondaonmain.com

Los Barrios
losbarrios1.com

Nicha's Comida Mexicana
nichas.com

Rosario's
rosariossa.com

Teka Molino
tekamolino.com

ORDER YOURSELF SOME ONION RINGS AND A MALT
AT THE MALT HOUSE

Just before Elvira Cisneros, mother of former Mayor Henry Cisneros, passed away, she requested food from the Malt House, a West Side institution since 1949. After you've tasted the Malt House's onion rings, you'll understand why. My mother-in-love and I dropped into the Malt House for lunch on our way to the San Fernando Cemetery Number Two. The restaurant has an extensive menu, but we both decided to order burgers, fries, chocolate malts, and a side of onion rings. The gentlemen at the table next to us had been eating at the Malt House since they were children. Mondays through Thursdays from 3 p.m. to 11 p.m., the Malt House offers two pieces of white meat, fries, and a medium drink for $3.95 on to-go orders. The real test, however, was their signature drink. After all, this is the Malt House. My MIL and I both drained ours to the very last drop and wished for more.

115 S Zarzamora, 210-433-8441
themalthouse.cc

LIVE LA VIDA LOCA(VORE)

The locavore movement—eating food that's grown within a hundred-mile radius of where it is purchased—is a national phenomenon that was dreamed up by three San Francisco-area women in 2005. Being a locavore helps reduce greenhouse gas emissions and supports local farmers. Plus, the food tastes great. It isn't processed, and most is organic, which means uncontaminated by pesticides. San Antonio chefs have jumped on board the locavore movement. Here are five restaurants that make their Mother (Earth) proud:

Restaurant Gwendolyn
restaurantgwendolyn.com

The Clean Plate
thecleanplatesanantonio.com

Southerleigh
southerleigh.com

Cured
curedatpearl.com

Pharm Table
pharmtable.com

YOU WON'T GO HUNGRY
(OR THIRSTY) AT PEARL

When the Culinary Institute of America opened up a branch in San Antonio at Pearl, a twenty-three-acre site along the Museum Reach of the River Walk at the former Pearl Brewery, the food scene in San Antonio exploded. The CIA's student-staffed restaurant, Nao, features Latin and South American food. Il Sogno Osteria, Chef Andrew Weissman's Italian restaurant, was featured in the *New York Times'* "36 Hours in San Antonio" travel section. Add The Sandbar Fish House and Market, Supper, Green Vegetarian Cuisine, Bakery Lorraine, La Gloria, Cured, Southerleigh, and Boiler House to Pearl's growing list of restaurants, bakeries, cafes, and bars, and choosing where to eat becomes a problem. Plus, farmers and foodies within a 150-mile radius of the Alamo City set up booths filled with vegetables, fresh eggs, cut flowers, baked goods, herbs, cheeses, bison, coffee, chocolates, lavender, and more every Saturday from 9 a.m. until 1 p.m. and Sunday from 10 a.m. until 2 p.m. Rain or shine.

303 Pearl Parkway, 210-212-7260
atpearl.com/food

SAVOR SAN ANTONIO'S SKYLINE
BEFORE ENJOYING A BIEN FRIA (COLD ONE)

The Hays Street Bridge, a Texas Civil Engineering Landmark built in 1881, spent the first part of its life spanning the Nueces River west of Uvalde before it was moved to San Antonio and erected in 1910 to provide a railroad track-free crossing from the East Side of San Antonio to downtown. The bridge, composed of two wrought iron truss spans, was closed in 1982 for safety reasons. It reopened to pedestrian and bicycle traffic in 2010, one hundred years after it made its San Antonio debut, thanks to the Herculean efforts of the Hays Street Bridge Restoration Group. Photo opportunities abound at this East Side landmark, so bring a camera. After you're done soaking up the views of downtown San Antonio, treat yourself to a locally brewed Alamo Beer just beneath the bridge. Alamo's beer garden and beer hall is open to the public Thursdays through Sundays and offers live music and food trucks.

803 N Cherry St.
facebook.com/Hays-Street-Bridge-151580447463/

GRAB A SLICE
(OR TWO OR THREE) OF PIZZA

San Antonio's Italian heritage is deeper than most realize. The local Christopher Columbus Italian Society was chartered in 1890, and San Francesco di Paolo Catholic Church was built in 1927 at 205 Piazza Italia off downtown's Martin Street. Even if you don't have an ounce of Italian blood in you, we're all Italian when it comes to pizza. Here's an alpha-ordered list of a dozen local establishments that will make your life *molto bene*!

Barbaro
barbarosanantonio.com

Big Lou's Pizza
biglouspizza-satx.com

Braza Brava Pizza Napoletana
facebook.com/BrazaBrava

Deco Pizzeria
decopizza.com

Dough Pizzeria Napoletana
doughpizzeria.com

Florio's Pizza
floriospizza.com

Guillermo's
guillermosdowntown.com

Il Sogno Osteria
visitsanantonio.com/Browse-Book/Dining/Il-Sogno

Julian's Italian Pizzeria and Kitchen
julianspizzeria.com

SOBRO Pizza Co.
sobropizza.com

Sorrento Ristorante
sorrentopizzeria.com

Stella Public House
stellapublichouse.com/location/san-antonio-2

SIP A BREW OR TWO
AT VFW POST 76, THE OLDEST IN TEXAS

Even though the VFW Post 76 is the oldest in Texas and was founded by veterans of the Spanish-American War, it was hidden from sight until the Museum Reach opened in 2009. The post was one of San Antonio's best-kept secrets. Not any more. Strolling along the River Walk from downtown toward the San Antonio Museum of Art or from Pearl toward downtown, natives and visitors encounter the majestic 1902 Victorian home nestled along the banks of the San Antonio River. On a Friday or a Saturday night, the festive crowd and live music will draw you in. The post's canteen is open daily. You don't have to be a veteran to enter VFW Post 76 or to purchase a brew, but you will have the opportunity to rub elbows with veterans of World War II, Korea, Vietnam, the Persian Gulf, Afghanistan, and Iraq and thank them for their service.

10 10th St., 210-223-4581
vfwpost76ontheriverwalk.org

CRUISE ART GALLERIES,
HISTORIC HOMES, AND GREAT EATS
IN SOUTHTOWN

Southtown, the neighborhood just south of downtown, came onto my radar when the Blue Star Contemporary Art Museum got its start in a warehouse along the San Antonio River back in 1986. H-E-B relocated its corporate headquarters to the area in 1985, San Angel Folk Art Gallery came along in 1989, and then came the expansion of the King William Fair during Fiesta, revitalization of King William's historic homes, First Friday art walks, the Blue Star Brewing Company, and you get the idea. Southtown was abuzz and still is. In addition to the arts and historic homes, this part of town is becoming known as a foodie paradise. People who live in the 'hood recommend the following culinary establishments:

Feast, feastsa.com

The Guenther House, guentherhouse.com

La Tuna Grill and La Tuna Icehouse, latunagrill.com

Liberty Bar, liberty-bar.com

Madhatters Tea House & Café, madhatterstea.com

Tito's Mexican Restaurant, titosrestaurant.com

TREAT YOURSELF AND YOUR SWEETIE
TO A ROMANTIC REPAST

San Antonio is the most romantic city in the United States of America, so it's no surprise that the Alamo City has a surfeit of seductive restaurants to help turn up the heat in both new and established relationships. I asked my fellow San Antonio bloggers (@SATXBloggers on Twitter) for their top romantic restaurants, and we came up with this list of swoon-worthy favorites:

Azúca
azuca.net

Biga on the Banks
biga.com

Bliss
foodisbliss.com

Bohanan's
bohanans.com

Cappy's
cappysrestaurant.com

Fig Tree Restaurant
dine.figtreerestaurant.com

Grey Moss Inn
grey-moss-inn.com

Las Canarias
omnihotels.com/hotels/san-antonio-la-mansion-del-rio/
dining/las-canarias

Little Italy
littleitalyrestaurantmenu.com

Tong's Thai
tongsthai.com

DON'T BE LIKE PRESIDENT FORD!
REMOVE THE HUSK

Even though I grew up in Southeast Texas where Latino anything was scarce, I was raised by parents who loved traveling to Mexico and loved Mexican food. Because of this childhood experience, I pick up a dozen tamales now and again to bring home to my own family. San Antonio, unlike my birthplace, is full of tamale vendors. In the more than thirty years I've lived here, I've tried quite a few. My favorite tamales, however, come from Adelita Tamales & Tortilla Factory. Four generations of the Borrego family and their employees have been making tamales, tortillas, chips, buñuelos, and more since 1938. For $7.75, you can get a dozen bean and jalapeño tamales to go. Pork or pork with jalapeño will run you $8.25, and a dozen chicken tamales are $9. Pork tamales are their best sellers. Their homemade masa is the real deal, and you can taste the difference in their tamales.

1130 Fresno, 210-733-5352
adelitatamales.com

STEP BACK IN TIME
AT SAN ANTONIO'S OLDEST BAR

The Menger Bar at the Menger Hotel is the oldest continuously operating saloon in San Antonio's history, according to a plaque outside its front door, which is a stone's throw from the Alamo. Opened in 1859, it was made into an exact replica of a pub in London's House of Lords in 1887. The Rough Rider Bar's name is derived from the time that Theodore "Teddy" Roosevelt enlisted recruits at the bar to fight in the 1898 Spanish-American War. With a maximum occupancy of sixty-five, the bar is extremely intimate. Memorabilia from the First Texas Cavalry on the Border (1916–1917) are on display along with a giant moose head and drawings of Teddy. Ask the bartender for a whiskey, and raise a glass to President Roosevelt for prioritizing and expanding America's national park system.

204 Alamo Plaza, 210-223-4361
mengerhotel.com/restaurants

MUSIC AND ENTERTAINMENT

CATCH A SHOW
AT THE TOBIN CENTER FOR THE PERFORMING ARTS

The Tobin Center is home to three of San Antonio's premier performing arts groups: the San Antonio Symphony, Ballet San Antonio, and Opera San Antonio. With another seven resident performing arts organizations in its stable and a supersized list of outside talent, the Tobin offers something for everyone. Located in downtown San Antonio along the Museum Reach of the River Walk, the Tobin Center was transformed from the Municipal Auditorium into its current $203-million incarnation with three separate venues: the H-E-B Performance Hall with seats for 1,738; the Carlos Alvarez Studio Theater, a smaller space with 240 seats; and the River Walk Plaza, an outdoor amphitheater that has space for 1,200 standing or 600 seated along with a 32-foot video wall that allows events inside to be simulcast outside. At night, the Tobin's AT&T Sky Wall lights up the center's silhouette, giving those of us who are crazy for San Antonio's annual River Walk Christmas lights a year-round fix.

100 Auditorium Circle, 210-223-8624
tobincenter.org

TRANSPORT YOURSELF
INTO ANOTHER WORLD AT THE MAJESTIC THEATRE

Some of the best concerts I've ever attended were in the Majestic Theatre: Stevie Ray Vaughan, James Taylor, Sade, Kenny Loggins, Basia, Little Feat, and ZZ Top to name just a few. In addition, I've thrilled to the traveling Broadway shows of *The Lion King*, *Cats*, *Wicked*, *Annie*, *12 Angry Men*, and *Beauty and the Beast* at the Majestic. Some of the movie *Selena* with Jennifer Lopez was filmed here. Yes, performing artists draw patrons into this 2,300-seat theatre, but the venue itself is another draw. The 1929 Mediterranean-style theatre designed by John Eberson is an over-the-top Baroque fantasy that's listed on the National Register of Historic Places and is a National Historic Landmark. I get a charge every time I walk through the Majestic's doors. I never tire of checking out the fish in the aquarium, people-watching in the multilevel atrium, and gazing up at the ceiling's twinkling stars. If you haven't been to the Majestic, what are you waiting on?

224 E Houston St., 210-226-5700
majesticempire.com

GET YOUR CUMBIA GROOVE ON
WITH BOMBASTA BARRIO BIG BAND

San Antonio has its share of first-rate live bands, but if you have to pick just one to experience before you die, you must choose Bombasta Barrio Big Band. I first heard Roberto Ybañez Livar and his eight bandmates at PACfest, Palo Alto College's official Fiesta event. I was blown away by their fusion of cumbia, hip hop, funk, rock, and Latin jazz. Since then, I've seen them perform at various locations around town, including Pearl's River Walk amphitheater. They never disappoint. Follow Bombasta on Facebook or Twitter or both so you don't miss a single performance. Hearing their music will lift your soul and transform avowed nondancers into hip-shaking hoofers. Shakira will have nothing on you.

youtu.be/9923Ei6gjAU
bombasta.com

EXPERIENCE
THE MAGIC OF LIVE MUSIC

The live music scene in San Antonio is strong. In addition to being able to catch major touring acts that appear at the Tobin Center, the AT&T Center, the Alamodome, the Majestic, the Empire, and the Aztec, you can also get up close and personal with top-notch musicians at smaller venues here in the Alamo City. (For additional live music options, check out festivals, page 86; dancing recs, page 88; the Guadalupe, page 41; the Carver, page 39; the Flea Mart, page 118; VFW Post 76, page 74; and the Arneson River Theater, page 8.) If you had to pick just five of all the live music venues in the region, you can't go wrong with the following:

Sam's Burger Joint
samsburgerjoint.com

The Cove
thecove.us

John T. Floore Country Store
liveatfloores.com

Gruene Hall
gruenehall.com

The St. Mary's Strip (Paper Tiger, Limelight,
Tycoon Flats, Hi-Tones, The Mix, and The Amp Room)
on North St. Mary's Street, between 281 and East Dewey Place

● ●

ATTEND
ONE OF SAN ANTONIO'S
LIFE-AFFIRMING FESTIVALS

Music. Food. Dancing. FUN! We're San Antonio, and you're invited to celebrate the fabulousness that is the Alamo City year-round.

Asian Festival
texancultures.com/festivals_events

Irish Festival
harpandshamrock.org/stpats.php

Maverick Music Festival
facebook.com/MaverickMusicFest

Fiesta
fiesta-sa.org

Cinco de Mayo
facebook.com/marketsquaresa

Tejano Conjunto Festival
guadalupeculturalarts.org/tejano-conjunto-festival

Gospel and Soul Food Festival
lavillitaheritage.com/have-you-got-soul

Summer Art and Jazz Festival
sanantoniosummerartjazzfestival.com/jazz

Texas Folklife Festival
texancultures.com/festivals_events

Fourth of July Celebration
saparksfoundation.org/events/
4th-of-july-celebration

Balcones Heights Jazz Festival
facebook.com/BalconesHeightsJazzFestival

International Accordion Festival
internationalaccordionfestival.org

Diez y Seis
facebook.com/marketsquaresa

Jazz'SAlive
saparksfoundation.org/events/jazzsalive

Oktoberfest
facebook.com/the.Beethoven

Luminaria
luminariasa.org

Diwali Festival of Lights
diwalisa.com

Mariachi Vargas Extravaganza
mariachimusic.com

Celebrate San Antonio
saparksfoundation.org/events/celebrate-san-antonio

DANCE THE NIGHT AWAY

San Antonio's dance club scene is rich with possibilities: techno, house, hip hop, country, new wave, industrial, salsa, bachata, merengue, and more. The three clubs you should not miss, however, were chosen with variety in mind. The Bonham Exchange in downtown San Antonio, close to the Alamo, is a progressive, gay-friendly establishment that opened in 1981. Its 1892 building is alone worth the price of admission. Cowboys DanceHall on the city's Northeast Side is a cavernous place that reminds visitors that everything is bigger in Texas. For those who want to get their Urban Cowboy and Cowgirl on, this is the place for you. Luna is a small, intimate venue with a Rat Pack vibe. Salsa, soul, R&B, Latin fusion, rockabilly, and more round out their live music scene. The music, tasty bar snacks, and affordable house cocktails make this North Side establishment a winner.

Bonham Exchange: bonhamexchange.com
Cowboys DanceHall: cowboysdancehall.com
Luna: lunalive.com

ESCAPE INTO AN ALTERNATE UNIVERSE
AT ONE OF SAN ANTONIO'S THEATRES

Drama. Comedy. Musicals. Tragedy. Improvisation. The Alamo City has it all. When the lights are dimmed and the curtain goes up, local playwrights, directors, actors, and techies pour their hearts and souls into revealing life's truths to the gathered audience. Notable San Antonio theatres include AtticRep, The Classic Theatre, Harlequin Dinner Theatre, Jump-Start Performance Co., The Overtime Theater, Sheldon Vexler Theatre, The Magik Theatre, The Playhouse (Russell Hill Rogers and Cellar Theaters), and Woodlawn Theatre. In addition to these, local colleges and universities have their own theatre departments. Treat yourself to a show!

satheatre.com

SPORTS AND RECREATION

LET YOUR RIPARIAN NATURE LOOSE
ON THE BANKS OF THE SAN ANTONIO RIVER

The Mission Reach Ecosystem Restoration and Recreation Project makes me weep tears of joy. Completed in 2013, the River Walk now extends from downtown to just below Loop 410, an eight-mile stretch that encompasses the South Side's four Spanish colonial missions. Walking, bicycle riding, and kayaking along these riparian wetlands is now a reality. For someone who lived in Austin for six years and maximized advantage of the hike and bike trail along Lady Bird Lake, this extension is a dream come true. Springtime is phenomenal. Bluebonnets, the state flower of Texas, line the trail. Native wildlife, such as blue-winged teals, green herons, and red-shouldered hawks, are present throughout the year. The $358-million project was definitely taxpayer money well spent. For those who'd like to roll down the reach, bicycles (B-Cycle and Blue Star Bike Shop) are available for rental at the Blue Star Arts Complex. For those who'd like to paddle, kayaks may be rented at Espada Park from Mission Kayak.

sanantonioriver.org/mission_reach/mission_reach

STRETCH YOUR LEGS
ALONG THE MUSEUM REACH
OF THE RIVER WALK

When my sister, good friend, and I were in France back in 1990, we shared a bottle of wine with an elderly man, a World War II veteran, whose brother now lives in the United States. He became verklempt while talking to us in his broken English. "Eets just so beautiful!" he exclaimed, wiping a tear from his eye. That's exactly how I feel about the extension of the River Walk from downtown all the way to Hildebrand Avenue. The Museum Reach is another hanky-producing happy cry. Thank you, city and county leaders, for making it and the Mission Reach so! From downtown, start your stroll at the Tobin Center for the Performing Arts and head north to Pearl. On the way, be sure to stop in at the San Antonio Museum of Art. The Witte Museum, Brackenridge Park, and the San Antonio Zoo and Aquarium are also along this stretch. Is San Antonio great or what?!

sanantonioriver.org/museum_reach/museum_reach

CREATE LIFELONG MEMORIES
AT AMERICA'S OLDEST CHILDREN'S AMUSEMENT PARK

Generation after generation of San Antonio's children have experienced fun times at Kiddie Park, which opened its gates in 1925. It features eight rides—carousel, ferris wheel, planes, boats, trains, helicopters, flying saucers, and pony rides—that will thrill the toddler- to-elementary-school-aged set. Children will also be able to enjoy pony rides on the weekends and ice skating during the winter months along with arcade and carnival games throughout the year. Renovated in 2009, Kiddie Park is a happy place that's perfect for snapping treasured family photos. Snack on cotton candy, popcorn, or ice cream while you're there.

3015 Broadway, 210-824-4351
kiddiepark.com

ESCAPE INTO NATURE
AT BRACKENRIDGE PARK NEAR DOWNTOWN SAN ANTONIO

Brackenridge Park is yet another of San Antonio's rejuvenating urban oases. Minutes from the center of downtown, you will find yourself surrounded by tall trees and a less-traveled stretch of the San Antonio River. The 344-acre park underwent a major renovation not long ago, and three walking trails opened to the public: Waterworks (1.5 miles), Wildlife (1 mile), and Wilderness (.75 mile). Public art may be found along each trail, and inviting picnic tables dot the landscape. The San Antonio Zoo and the San Antonio Zoo Eagle, a miniature train, are also located in the park. However, when you need a place to clear your head and commune with some koi, head over to the park's Sunken Gardens, officially named the San Antonio Japanese Tea Garden. You can make your visit a two-for-one (gardens/zoo), three-for-one (gardens/zoo/miniature train), or four-for-one (gardens/zoo/miniature train/park) adventure. Notice, however, that the gardens are a given. Don't miss them! Admission to the gardens is free.

3700 N St. Mary's, 210-207-8480
sanantonio.gov/ParksAndRec

● ●

VISIT
ONE OF THE NATION'S OLDEST PARKS, SAN PEDRO SPRINGS

Stroll through San Pedro Springs Park, San Antonio's oldest park and the second-oldest park in the nation. According to historians, Native Americans gathered at San Pedro Springs and Creek more than twelve thousand years ago, and the Spaniards settled here in the early 1700s. Stunning cypress trees line the artistically designed pool that looks like it's spring fed, but it's not. Therefore, you won't freeze your you-know-whats off like you do at Barton Springs in Austin. The real springs are visible just north of the pool, but you're not supposed to swim in them because of the potential damage you may cause. The pool is run by the City of San Antonio and is open during the summer months. Admission is free, but you do have to wear proper swimming attire to get in. During the rest of the year, enjoy a picnic at one of the many tables or benches.

1415 San Pedro Ave., 210-207-7275
sanantonio.gov/ParksAndRec

SAY "SÍ!" ("YES!")
TO FITNESS AT SÍCLOVÍA

Síclovía, San Antonio's spin on Bógota, Columbia's Ciclovía, started in October 2011, making two miles of Broadway car-free for folks to enjoy outdoor recreational sports and activities without having to worry about being run over. Skateboarders, walkers, runners, hula hoopers, skaters, tricyclers, bicyclers, bubble-blowers, strollers, scooters, and dog lovers look forward to this free twice-per-year event. Síclovía's slogan "Go play in the street!" should add (and parks) in parentheses. The YMCA sets up stages along the route to give attendees a taste of Zumba, kickboxing, Pilates, and more. Down Broadway at Lions Field, hula hoops were at the ready, along with giant chess boards and bubble wands. A tae kwon do presentation was in full swing, demonstrating this South Korean martial art. Some years, you can even Zumba at the Alamo! Routes vary each Síclovía, so check their website. Kick-start your path to fitness at this fun, family-friendly event.

ymcasatx.org/siclovia

PLAY A ROUND OR TWO
AT THE "WORLD'S FINEST" MINIATURE GOLF COURSE, COOL CREST

Cool Crest Miniature Golf Course claims to be the World's Finest, and who's to argue with them? Set atop the apex of Fredericksburg Road within sight of Interstate 10, this tropical paradise has been a San Antonio recreational staple since 1929. Two eighteen-hole courses are challenging, yet fun. I had a pretty good run until I got to not-so-lucky hole thirteen and hole fourteen, which ran uphill. Despite these two setbacks, my overall score was decent. As the encouraging lady at the front desk said when I returned my putter, "Practice makes perfect!" Harold and Maria Metzger ran Cool Crest for almost seventy years. In 2013, the Andry family took over, and they've continued in the Metzgers' footsteps. Why mess with the world's finest?! The beautiful landscaping draws a variety of butterflies and is a welcome antidote to screen time overload. Losers have to treat the winners to a paleta from El Paraiso up the road!

1402 Fredericksburg Rd., 210-732-0222
coolcrestgolf.com

PAINT YOUR FACE FOR COLLEGE BALL

The Valero Alamo Bowl has been providing zealous fans a college football fix since 1993. The second-choice team of the Pac-12 Conference goes up against the third-choice team of the Big 12 Conference in late December or early January at the downtown Alamodome, which seats sixty-five thousand. Over the years, UCLA has tangled with Kansas State, TCU beat Oregon, and Baylor triumphed over Washington. More than one thousand high school musicians, dancers, and cheerleaders wow at the halftime show. To take advantage of the Alamo Bowl's holiday time period, the event's organizers have prepared a Bowl Week itinerary to maximize your stay in the Alamo City. Check out their website. Whether your team is in the game or not, a good time is guaranteed.

100 Montana St., 210-226-2695
alamobowl.com

TAKE IN A SPURS GAME
AT THE AT&T CENTER

When a friend was in Madrid, Spain, he and his family wandered into a prohibited military area. Before they realized their mistake, the Guardia Civil, the city's police force, surrounded them. My friend, a former Marine who speaks Spanish, raised his hands over his head and said, "Lo siento. No somos de aqui. Somos de San Antonio, Texas." (We're sorry. We're not from here. We're from San Antonio, Texas.) One of the guards smiled and replied, "Los Spurs!" Yes, the San Antonio Spurs have put the Alamo City on the world's map. With an international set of players along with those from the U.S., the National Basketball Association champions make San Antonio proud. Coach Gregg "Pop" Popovich has brought out the best in the team since 1996. The players are known for being gentlemen both on and off of the court. From the end of October through April, don't miss your opportunity to witness greatness in action. ¡Viva Los Spurs!

1 AT&T Center Parkway, 210-444-5000
nba.com/spurs/tickets

GET YOUR FILL
OF BRONC RIDERS AND BARREL RACERS AT THE STOCK SHOW & RODEO

If it's February, it must be the rodeo! Trail riders from across the state make their way to this Texas-sized event, rain or shine. The San Antonio Stock Show & Rodeo is one of the country's largest with attendance that tops a million and a half. More than six thousand volunteers make it happen. Every year since 2005 it's won the Professional Rodeo Cowboys Association's Large Rodeo of the Year Award. Over a three-week period, attendees enjoy bronc and bull riders, barrel racers, and mutton busters along with top-rate entertainment. More than $160 million has been given to youth in Texas through scholarships, grants, calf scrambles, and show premiums since 1984. In the livestock barns, visitors can commune with beef cattle, dairy cattle, chickens, turkeys, goats, pigs, and sheep. Visitors will also enjoy an on-site carnival, pony rides, a petting zoo, a swine sprint, shopping, and food. If you've never had a bucking bull almost land in your lap, you haven't lived.

723 AT&T Center Parkway, 210-225-5851
sarodeo.com

LET YOUR SPIRIT SOAR
AT MORGAN'S WONDERLAND

Morgan's Wonderland is the world's first theme park designed for individuals with special needs. The Hartman Family Foundation created the park so that people with and without disabilities can come together to have fun and learn how to understand each other better. The $34-million outdoor park features rides, playgrounds, gardens, a catch-and-release fishing lake, a miniature train, an amphitheater, and picnic areas that are all wheelchair accessible. A multimillion dollar water park will open in Spring 2017. The twenty-five-acre park opened in 2010 and already has hosted guests from all fifty states as well as fifty-five countries. Entry into Morgan's Wonderland is a bargain! People with special needs and children under the age of three are admitted without charge. Tickets for children ages three to eleven, seniors ages sixty-two and above, and military are $11. Adults tickets are $17. Parking is free.

5223 David Edwards Dr., 210-495-5888
morganswonderland.com

RUN 26.2 OR 13.1 OR 6.2 OR 3.1 MILES
AT SAN ANTONIO'S
ROCK 'N' ROLL MARATHON

More than thirty Rock 'n' Roll Marathons are held around the world, but San Antonio's is the only one that has the Alamo on its route. Trinity University, King William, Mission San Jose, and the Mission Reach portion of the River Walk are also included. Live bands, cheerleaders, and an army of volunteers give the thirty thousand participants the lift they need to make it across the finish line and into the party and headliner concert at the Alamodome. Not a runner? No problem! You may also walk. Dancing is optional.

runrocknroll.com/san-antonio

RELEASE YOUR INNER CHILD
AT YANAGUANA GARDEN

Hemisfair Park, the site of the 1968 World's Fair that celebrated San Antonio's 250th birthday, is undergoing a $30-million renovation to turn itself into a world-class urban park in downtown San Antonio. Yanaguana Garden, an outdoor play area for both children and adults, is the first area of the park to reopen. Nestled along César Chávez Boulevard and South Alamo Street, the four-acre park features a Parc Güell-like giant blue panther covered in mosaic tiles and glass beads by local artist Oscar Alvarado. The Pantera Azul begs to be climbed and photographed. Seven additional local artists joined in creating this engaging space that includes a giant sandbox, a splash pad, climbing structures, a performance-ready stage, and more. Hemisfair Park is open seven days a week from 7 a.m. until midnight.

434 S Alamo St.
hemisfair.org
facebook.com/HemisfairSanAntonio

LEARN HOW
TO WALK LIKE A PENGUIN AT SEAWORLD OF SAN ANTONIO

Shamu gets top billing at SeaWorld of San Antonio, but I personally find the penguins in their frosty habitat pretty hard to beat! If penguins aren't your thing, dolphins, sea lions, alligators, flamingos, belugas, and more are at the ready. Eight big-production shows and six spine-tingling rides, including The Great White and Steel Eel, will keep you hopping. If that's not enough, you may want to purchase an add-on Aquatica water park ticket. Restaurants and concession stands are located throughout the park, but you might want to consider packing a lunch to eat outside of the entrance. You might also consider taking the #64 VIA bus to avoid the $20 parking fee. SeaWorld is big, so be sure to wear comfortable shoes.

10500 Sea World Dr., 210-523-3000
seaworldparks.com/seaworld-sanantonio

HOLD ON TIGHT
AT SIX FLAGS FIESTA TEXAS

Six Flags Fiesta Texas is known for its nine scream-inducing roller-coasters: Batman, Boomerang, Goliath, Iron Rattler, Kiddee Koaster, Pandemonium, Poltergeist, Road Runner, and Superman Krypton Coaster. (And more are on the way!) For those who are roller-coaster averse, the two-hundred-acre park also offers forty other rides, a water park that includes a Texas-shaped wave pool, live entertainment, food, and shopping. Six Flags Fiesta Texas stages various events throughout the year, such as Spring Break, Fourth of July, Halloween, and the holidays to name a few. To save some money, buy your tickets and parking online. VIA's #94 Fiesta Texas Express runs from downtown. All ages, from grandkids to grandparents, will enjoy this family-friendly park that is located in a former rock quarry.

17000 IH-10 West, 210-697-5050
sixflags.com/fiestatexas

VISIT
THE LARGEST UNDERGROUND CAVERNS IN TEXAS

The odds of most of us traveling into space are pretty slim, but traveling into Earth is within our reach. Just thirty minutes from the Alamo, Natural Bridge Caverns gives explorers a chance to venture 180 feet below ground and finally learn the difference between stalactites and stalagmites. Choose one of four underground tours. Ancient formations, including flowstones, chandeliers, totem poles, fried eggs, soda straws, and the sixty-foot limestone slab bridge, will inspire awe. Wear rubber-soled shoes with good tread, as the pathways can be slippery. Strollers are not recommended. If you're feeling adventuresome after all that time below ground, give the Canopy Zip Line a try.

26495 Natural Bridge Caverns Rd., 210-651-6101
naturalbridgecaverns.com

COMMUNE WITH NATURE
AND WORK UP A SWEAT

In addition to all of San Antonio's city parks, the Alamo City is fortunate to have eight natural areas or preserves within its city limits: Crownridge Canyon, Eisenhower Park, Friedrich Wilderness Park, Government Canyon, Phil Hardberger, Medina River, Panther Springs, and Walker Ranch Historic Landmark Park. Crownridge's 207 acres, part of the Edwards Aquifer Protection Program initiative, offers hillside vistas and forested canyon bottoms. Friedrich, home of the endangered Golden-cheeked Warbler, offers 5.5 miles of hiking. Government Canyon, a state natural area, is located on more than seventy-five-hundred acres of the aquifer's recharge zone and has more than forty miles of trails. The South Side's Medina River Natural Area is a 511-acre preserve along the banks of what was once the official boundary between Texas and Mexico. Phil Hardberger covers more than three hundred acres on the city's North Side with one of the best dog parks in town. And don't forget the Mitchell Lake Audubon Center, a 1,200-acre natural area on the South Side. In other words, grab your tennis shoes and a reusable water bottle! You have acres and acres to explore.

sanantonio.gov/ParksAndRec/ParksFacilities/AllParksFacilities/
A-ZParksFacilitiesIndex.aspx
tpwd.texas.gov/state-parks/government-canyon
sanaturalareas.org
mitchelllake.audubon.org

SHOPPING AND FASHION

SEARCH FOR A PERFECT GIFT
AT FIESTA ON MAIN

When my childhood friend's grandmother would bemoan an unsuccessful shopping trip, she'd sniff, "I didn't even open my purse." This will not be your problem at Fiesta on Main, a store whose motto "Where Mexico is closer than you think, and Fiesta never ends!" is an understatement. Fiesta on Main specializes in folk art, talavera pottery, Fiesta decorations, piñatas, paper flowers, flower garland crowns, papel picado, confetti eggs, furniture, wedding decorations, Day of the Dead items, Christmas decorations, clothing, and more. "And more" does not begin to address their inventory. Fiesta on Main is not for minimalists. Every square inch of space is crammed with something wonderful that you will want to bring home with you or give to a friend. My maternal grandmother's maxim comes to mind: "Don't buy anything you need, darlin'. Just buy something you want." You'll find plenty you want at Fiesta on Main, and for out-of-town guests, one-stop souvenir shopping has never been easier.

2025 N Main Ave., 210-738-1188
alamofiesta.com

FEED YOUR CREATIVITY
AT LAS COLCHAS

If you want to lower your blood pressure and recharge your creative batteries, Las Colchas is the place for you. Even if you've never handled a needle and thread in your life, you'll be welcomed and inspired by this quaint quilt shop tucked away in downtown San Antonio. It's always a joy just to walk in to see what's on display. Plus, the owners, Francine and Toni, always have coffee and treats set out for their guests. What's not to like about that?! Las Colchas has fabric to suit every taste: traditional (Civil War era), Tex-Mex (*Dia de Los Muertos*), modern (Kaffee Fasset), international (Japanese), and more. Plus, they have ready-made kits for those who don't have a clue how to get started. I've taken four classes at Las Colchas: crazy quilt, vintage embroidery, prayer flags, and punched embroidery. From each class, I walked away with a handmade treasure to enjoy now before passing it on to the next generation. What will you make?

110 Ogden St., 210-223-2405
lascolchas.com

CHECK OUT THE WORLD'S LARGEST COWBOY BOOTS
AT NORTH STAR MALL

San Antonio, like every large city, has its share of shopping destinations, but North Star Mall is the only place that has a giant pair of cowboy boots set out to welcome you. North Star turned fifty in 2010, and it has aged well. Anchored by Macy's, Dillard's, Saks Fifth Avenue, JCPenney, and Forever 21, North Star Mall has approximately two hundred tenants. H&M, Abercrombie & Fitch, Michael Kors, Kate Spade, the Disney Store, Gap, J.Crew, Talbots, Victoria's Secret, Armani Exchange, Fossil, GUESS, Nine West, Steve Madden, Apple, Godiva Chocolatier, and more offer something to suit every age and disposition. According to Google maps, the distance between San Pedro and McCullough is approximately half of a mile, so you'll log a mile if you walk from one end of the mall and back, and that doesn't include detours along the way. Happy shopping! If North Star Mall doesn't quench your shopping thirst, give The Shops at La Cantera, located off of 1604 near Six Flags Fiesta Texas, a whirl.

7400 San Pedro Ave., 210-340-6627
northstarmall.com

FIND FASHION WITH A FLAIR
AT PAINTED PONY CLOTHING OUTLET

President/Owner Kathy Hoermann has been designing jackets that ship to boutiques across the United States for more than twenty years. The amazing thing is that Hoermann manufactures her Painted Pony jackets right here in San Antonio, Texas. Her "uniquely USA" corporate headquarters is located at 5619 San Pedro, where she allows shoppers who call ahead to purchase sample returns, overruns, and retired fabrics. (Quilter alert!) Their hours are Mondays through Thursdays from 8 a.m. until 4 p.m. and Fridays from 8 a.m. until 11:30 a.m. At the outlet, I picked up a wonderful green-on-green geometric print jacket from a sale rack for $25! Most of the jackets sell for $68, which is below wholesale. The employee who helped me said that she bought fifty jackets the first year she worked there. I can totally understand why. Hoermann has a real flair, and you're guaranteed compliments galore when you wear one of her designs.

5619 San Pedro, 210-377-3335
paintedpony.com

UNEARTH A TREASURE OR TWO
AT OFF MY ROCKER AND BOYSVILLE THRIFT STORE

San Antonio has its share of treasure-laden thrift and consignment stores. Two of my favorites are located within walking distance of each other on West Olmos Drive. San Antonio's decorators flock to Off My Rocker, a consignment store, to fluff up clients' nests. The owner, Jo Lynn, said she wants everyone to walk out of her store with something wonderful. Lord knows I've walked out with heaps of wonderfulness over the years—just ask my husband. He shakes his head every time I walk into the house with another bag from OMR. Another place I never walk out empty-handed is Boysville Thrift Store. Their slogan, "Find your treasure today!" totally fits. Furniture, art, fabric, knickknacks, jewelry, and carved wooden animals have all found a new home with me or my family and friends. Shopping here is a win-win. Your purchase benefits Boysville, a home for girls and boys in crisis situations. Let the hunt begin!

204 W Olmos Dr., offmyrockersa.com
307 W Olmos Dr., boysvillethriftstore.org

BEAT SANTA TO THE PUNCH
AT THE ESPERANZA PEACE MARKET

The Esperanza Peace and Justice Center's Annual Mercado de Paz is only open the two days after Thanksgiving each year. It was with great pleasure and awe that I encountered Irene Aguilar Alcántara, one of the famed Aguilar sisters, ceramic artists extraordinaire from Oaxaca, Mexico, at the Peace Market. My husband and I toured the Aguilar sisters' studios in Mexico in 2007, but there was only so much we could bring back on the plane. It was a real joy to be able to chat with Irene and buy *Frida Muerta*, a piece of her folk art, for a mere $20. Not all of the artists at the Mercado de Paz are from out of town. Many homegrown artists are also present. I spied an oh-so-wonderful brightly colored crocheted toque and HAD to have it, especially when I found out that it cost only $8. See what you'll find at the market, San Antonio's remedy for Black Friday!

922 San Pedro at Evergreen, 210-228-0201
esperanzacenter.org

BROWSE
'TIL YOUR HEART IS CONTENT
AT THE FLEA MART

You never know what you're going to find at a flea market, and that's half the fun. The other half is a combination of people-watching, corn-on-the-cob eating, and conjunto dancing. Although San Antonio has more than a dozen flea markets in the surrounding region, I suggest you head south to the Flea Mart on the Poteet Highway, just outside Loop 410. There you will find an enormous selection of piñatas, personalized T-shirts, quinceañera gowns, religious holy cards, Our Lady of Guadalupe key chains, and leather cowboy boots made in Guanajuato, Mexico. You may even purchase your own grave marker at the Flea Mart. Ice-cold beer, raspas (snow cones), and cotton candy make strolling around this paved and covered flea market even nicer. The Flea Mart is open every Saturday and Sunday from 10 a.m. until 6 p.m. Parking costs $2, but it's free before 10 a.m. Live conjunto music starts at noon both days.

12280 Poteet Jourdanton Freeway (Hwy. 16), 210-624-2666
fleamarketsanantonio.com

HUNT FOR GARDEN FAIRIES
AT SHADES OF GREEN

One of my friends goes to Shades of Green whenever she's feeling blue. "You just can't be sad there," she said. I have to agree. Shades of Green will put anyone in a good mood. Meandering pathways, soothing fountains, cedar arbors, and blooming flowers are sure to lift your spirits. It's a gardener's dream. Even if you're not a gardener, you'll want to become one. It's that inspiring. The knowledgeable, friendly staff at Shades of Green will teach you about native plants and the benefits of organic gardening while you're there, but if you'd like to learn more, their free Saturday seminars begin at 9:45 a.m. The coffee is on at 9 a.m. Looking for a perfect gift for your gardening friends and family? Shades of Green will have it. Be sure to put this neighborhood nursery on your feel-good list!

334 W Sunset Rd., 210-824-3772
shadesofgreensa.com

SUGGESTED
ITINERARIES

ARTS & CULTURE

PURO SAN ANTONIO

LONG WEEKEND GETAWAY

Arrive San Antonio on Thursday evening

Friday schedule

Haunted Tours of Downtown San Antonio, 6

The Esquire Tavern, 53

Saturday schedule

Breakfast at Il Sogno, 70

Pearl Farmers Market, 70

San Antonio Museum of Art, 4, 25, 93

Taco Cabana Happy Hour (Broadway near Mulberry location), 60

Brackenridge Park, 25, 95

San Antonio Zoo and Aquarium, 20, 25, 95

Japanese Gardens (also known as Sunken Gardens), 25, 95

Dinner at Augie's Barbed Wire Smokehouse or Demo's Greek Food, 57, 64

Sunday schedule

Mass at San Fernando Cathedral, 13

Breakfast Tacos at Panchito's, Taco Taco, Taco Garage, El Milagrito, or Pete's Tako House, 55

McNay Art Museum (opens at noon on Sunday), 4

Depart Sunday afternoon

HISTORY BUFF

The Alamo, 2

Mission Reach (Missions Concepción, San Jose, San Juan, and Espada), 11, 92

San Fernando Cathedral, 13

DOWNTOWN

NORTH

SOUTH

EAST

ACTIVITIES
BY SEASON

SPRING

St. Patrick's Day river-dyeing, 3, 86

San Antonio Book Festival, 5, 16

Fiesta, 23

Earth Day at Eco Centro, 32

San Antonio Botanical Garden, 17

Mission Reach, 92

Natural Areas and City Parks, 109

SUMMER

Paletas, 58

San Pedro Springs Swimming Pool, 96

Feast Day of St. Anthony de Padua (June 13), 18

SeaWorld, 105

Six Flags Fiesta Texas, 106

Texas Folklife Festival, 38, 86

Morgan's Wonderland, 102

Cool Crest Miniature Golf, 98

Art Museums and Galleries, 4

INDEX

• •

• •